GW01219957

This Book Belongs To

____

Copyright © Trendy Printing Library
All Rights Reserved

Trendy Printing
Library

Printed in Great Britain
by Amazon

82063224R10058